Incredible Fish

EXPRESS EDITION

John Townsend

www.raintreepublishers.co.uk
Visit our website to find out more information about **Raintree** books.

To order:
☎ Phone 44 (0) 1865 888113
▤ Send a fax to 44 (0) 1865 314091
▣ Visit the Raintree Bookshop at **www.raintreepublishers.co.uk** to browse our catalogue and order online.

First published in Great Britain by Raintree Publishers,
Halley Court, Jordan Hill, Oxford, OX2 8EJ,
part of Harcourt Education Ltd.
Raintree is a registered trademark of Harcourt
Education Ltd.

Produced for Raintree Publishers by Discovery Books Ltd
Editorial: Louise Galpine, Elisabeth Taylor,
Charlotte Guillain, and Diyan Leake
Expert Reader: Jill Bailey
Design: Victoria Bevan, Keith Williams (sprout.uk.com
Limited), and Michelle Lisseter
Picture Research: Maria Joannou
Production: Duncan Gilbert and Jonathan Smith
Printed and bound in China by South China
Printing Company
Originated by Repro Multi Warna

ISBN 1 844 43517 2 (hardback)
09 08 07 06 05
10 9 8 7 6 5 4 3 2 1

ISBN 1 844 43586 5 (paperback)
09 08 07 06 05
10 9 8 7 6 5 4 3 2 1

British Library Cataloguing in Publication Data
Townsend, John
Incredible fish. – (Freestyle express. Incredible creatures)
597
A full catalogue record for this book is available from the
British Library.

This levelled text is a version of Freestyle:
Incredible creatures: Incredible fish.

Photo acknowledgements
The publisher would like to thank the following for permission
to reproduce photographs: Ardea p. 30; Corbis pp. 6 top
(Robert Yin), 17 (Tim Wright), 48 (Jeffrey L. Rotman); FLPA
pp. 4–5, 9 left, 10–11, 11, 12–13, 13, 14, 16–17, 19 bottom,
19 top, 20, 22–3, 24, 25, 26 top, 34, 35, 36, 43, 45 top, 48–9,
50, 50–1, 52; Image Quest 3–D p. 41; NASA p. 46 (Jacques
Descloitres, MODIS Rapid Response Team, GSFC); Nature
Photo Library pp. 28 top (John Downer), 31; NHPA pp. 4, 5
top, 5 middle, 5 bottom, 6 bottom, 7, 8, 9 right, 10, 12, 15
bottom, 15 top, 16, 20–1, 22, 26 bottom, 27, 28 bottom, 29,
30–1, 33, 34–5, 37 top, 37 bottom, 38 left, 38–9, 39 right, 40,
40–1 (Bill Wood), 42–3, 42, 45 bottom, 44, 46–7, 47, 49;
Oxford Scientific Films pp. 18, 24–5, 32–3, 32 left;
Photofusion p. 51; Science Photo Library p. 23 (Alexis
Rosenfeld); www.jjphoto.dk p. 21

Cover photograph of a piranha reproduced with
permission of Getty Images (Image Bank)

The Publishers would like to thank Jon Pearce for his
assistance in the preparation of this book.

Every effort has been made to contact copyright holders
of any material reproduced in this book. Any omissions
will be rectified in subsequent printings if notice is given
to the Publishers.

Disclaimer
All the Internet addresses (URLs) given in this book were
valid at the time of going to press. However, due to the
dynamic nature of the Internet, some addresses may have
changed, or sites may have changed or ceased to exist since
publication. While the author and Publishers regret any
inconvenience this may cause readers, no responsibility for
any such changes can be accepted by either the author or
the Publishers.

Contents

Any words appearing in the text in bold, **like this**, are explained in the Glossary. You can also look out for some of them in the 'Wild words' bank at the bottom of each page.

Fantastic fish!

Fast fish

Tuna fish, swordfish and some sharks are fast fish. They can reach 80 kilometres (50 miles) per hour.

Fish live either in salty sea water or in freshwater lakes and rivers. Very few can live in both salty and fresh water. Most fish can only **survive** under water, but there are some that can live on land.

Almost all fish have fins and slimy **scales** to keep them **waterproof** and to protect them. But some do not. There are three main types of fish — bony fish, bendy fish, and jawless fish.

▲ **Shoals** of tuna dart through the sea at high speed.

scales small, bony plates that protect the skin on fish and reptiles

Bony fish have a skeleton made of bone. There are about 20,000 different **species** of bony fish. That is about 95 per cent of all fish.

Bendy fish, such as sharks and rays, have skeletons made of bendy **gristle**. This is the same material that makes up the shape of your nose. There are about 900 bendy fish. Nearly all of these live in the sea.

Jawless fish, such as lampreys and hagfish, do not have jaws or proper fins and tails. They are **parasites** with soft mouths that suck on other fish or the dead remains of animals.

Find out later...

... the greatest fish discovery of the 20th century.

... which fish has no teeth, but bites.

... which is the most shocking fish.

▲ The great white shark can open its jaws a metre wide.

species type of living animal or plant

Meet the family

Smallest

The smallest fish in the world is the dwarf goby. It is only 1 centimetre (half an inch) long.

Fins and scales

Most fish use fins to swim and steer. Fish are slippery and **streamlined** so they can move easily through water.

All fish are cold-blooded. This means they do not make their own body heat like **mammals**. They stay at the same temperature as the water around them.

Most fish are covered in scales to keep their bodies **waterproof** and protect them.

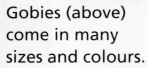

Gobies (above) come in many sizes and colours.

▲ This sea bass is streamlined and covered in **scales**.

streamlined smoothly shaped to move easily through water

Colours

Fish have many different colours and patterns. Some can **camouflage** themselves by changing colour to match their surroundings.

Fish that swim near the surface often have white bellies, silvery sides, and dark blue backs. This makes it difficult for **predators** to spot them. From above they look like the dark sea. While from below, they look like the paler sky.

▼ A diver is safe near the mouth of the whale shark. These fish do not attack humans.

Largest

The whale shark is the largest fish and it is almost 1500 times bigger than the dwarf goby. It can be as big as a bus and weigh up to 12 tonnes.

camouflage colours and patterns that match the background

▼ The rare coelacanth can live for up to 60 years.

Older than dinosaurs

An ancient fish called a coelacanth (say "see-la-kanth") lived before the dinosaurs. **Fossils** show that similar fish lived 400 million years ago.

Scientists thought the coelacanth had been **extinct** for a long time. Then, in 1938, one was found swimming in the Indian Ocean near Africa. Scientists believe that this one was just like its ancient **ancestors**. The **species** has not changed at all.

Sharp-nosed

The sailfish (below) is a sharp-nosed, fast swimmer. Like the marlin, it belongs to the swordfish family. It has a huge fin that stands up like a sail.

Fastest

Marlins are some of the fastest hunters in the sea. They can even fold away their fins into grooves in their bodies so they go faster. Marlins have long, pointed noses that slash like spears through tuna fish. They can grow to 4 metres (12 feet) long and live for about twenty years.

The fastest fish is the sailfish. It can reach a speed of 109 kilometres (68 miles) per hour.

fossil remains of a plant or animal that lived a very long time ago

Bendy

Some of the strongest and biggest fish have bendy skeletons. The skeletons are made of **gristle** instead of bone. Gristle is softer than bone.

Rays

Rays are flat fish with wide fins. They flap their fins like wings and glide gracefully along the seabed. Here they find shellfish and worms to eat. They can hide from **predators** by covering themselves with sand.

The bat ray's sting

The bat ray has two long fins that look like a bat's ears.

It can lash a predator with its long, thin tail. The spines on the tail inject poison into the attacker.

gristle strong, slightly bendy material, often called cartilage

Sharks

There are nearly 400 **species** of shark. The smallest is the spined pygmy shark which is 18 centimetres (7 inches) long. That is about the size of a hand. The huge whale shark is as long as a bus. It is 14 metres (45 feet) long.

All sharks eat meat but very few attack people. More people die from bee stings than shark attacks.

Hammerheads

The hammerhead has a wide, flat head with an eye at each end.

The shark also has thousands of tiny scent **receptors** along the edges of its head. These tell it when **prey** is near.

◄ Manta rays often rise to the surface of the ocean.

Amazing bodies

Gills

Gills are feathery flaps on the sides of a fish's head. They take oxygen from the water into the fish's blood.

Healthy gills are bright red because the blood in the gills is full of oxygen.

How do fish breathe under water?

Fish need **oxygen** to breathe, just like us. But they do not need air to breathe. There is plenty of oxygen in the water in seas and rivers. At least there should be. If water becomes polluted, there is not as much oxygen in it.

A fish constantly gulps in water through its mouth and passes it out through its **gills**. The gills take the oxygen into the fish's bloodstream.

▲ These gills of an Atlantic salmon are healthy and red.

▶ These fish have died because the water was polluted.

gills flaps on the side of a fish's head that are used for breathing

When fish cannot breathe

Most fish can only take oxygen from water. When small ponds nearly dry up, all the fish crowd into the water that is left. If they use up all the oxygen in the water, they "drown".

Plants that grow in water make oxygen. If water becomes **polluted** and plants die, there will not be enough oxygen for the fish. If they are short of oxygen, fish rise close to the surface to breathe.

Herbert the turbot

Some fish can **survive** for hours without breathing.

Michael Reeves caught a turbot in Dorset, England, in 2002. He took it home and put it in the fridge. Fifteen hours later Michael took the fish out to cook it. The turbot flapped a fin.

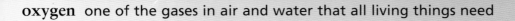

Lungfish

Some fish have lungs as well as **gills**. This means they can breathe on land as well as in water.

Lungfish live in lakes and rivers in Australia, South America, and Africa. They have long bodies and can **slither** across land. The African lungfish can grow to over 2 metres (6 feet) in length. That is the height of a man.

Teeth

Lungfish have very sharp teeth. They will attack anything that moves. It would be very risky to lift one out of the water.

▲ Lungfish can swim up to the surface and gulp air into their lungs.

slither slide along like a snake

Survival

When ponds dry up in the dry season, the African lungfish buries itself in the mud. It stays curled up until the tapping of rain wakes it.

The Queensland lungfish in Australia lifts its head up and breathes in air when its stream runs low. It can **survive** for only a few days without water.

▲ An African lungfish slithers across dry land.

Lungfish supper

In Africa, some people eat lungfish. How do they find them when they are buried in the mud?

They pretend to be rain by tapping on the ground with their fingers. The lungfish wake up. They think it is time to head for the pond.

survive stay alive despite danger and difficulties

Eels

It is hard to believe these snake-like animals are fish. Eels live in the sea as well as in fresh water. They like to be at the bottom of the sea or riverbed. They hide in the mud or under stones. Eels can also slither over land, rather like snakes.

As well as having **gills**, eels can also breathe through their skin. This means they can **survive** out of water too.

On land

Eels can travel miles over land in search of ponds and streams. They feed on worms, insects, and sometimes frogs.

▶ European eels can live up to 85 years.

Disappearing eels

European eels live in damp ditches, streams, and rivers. They are becoming rare because too many are caught for food.

The very young eels are known as glass eels. This is because they are see-through. **Poachers** catch them and sell them to eel farms. Herons and otters also eat European eels.

Swamped

Asian swamp eels were brought to Florida in the United States about ten years ago.

There are now tens of thousands of them. So many eels are a threat to the balance of nature in the Everglades National Park.

Feeding

Cod cleaners

Scavengers, such as cod, do a good job of clearing up the ocean.

When Australian fishermen cut open a huge cod in 2000, they found a man's head inside. Police thought the man had fallen into the water. Scavenging fish had eaten his body.

Fish feed in very different ways. Some are meat-eaters, some are **vegetarian**. Others eat both plants and animals. There are four different types of feeders.

Grazers eat seaweed and **algae**. These plants grow on rocks and shells on the seabed near the coast. Fish scrape the algae off with their mouths.

Scavengers are the cleaners of the ocean. They live on scraps of meat that have been dropped by killer fish. They also feed on the bodies of dead animals lying on the seabed.

▼ A diver meets a potato cod in Australia.

Wild words   scavenger animal that feeds on scraps and the prey of other animals

Killers are **predators**. They hunt smaller fish. They may swim long distances looking for their **prey**. They have sharp teeth and strong mouths to grab and tear prey.

Filter feeders filter the sea water to find their food. They suck up tiny animals and plants. Whale sharks feed like this, eating thousands of very tiny animals called **krill**.

Taste buds

Fish don't just have taste buds on the inside of their mouths like we do. They have them on the outside as well.

The catfish (above) also has taste buds on its whiskers. These help it to find food.

◄ This grazing damsel fish is picking algae from coral.

filter feeder animal that takes water into its body and strains out tiny pieces of food

Fish that bite

One of the largest freshwater fish is the giant catfish. It can be as long as a car and weigh up to 250 kilograms (550 pounds).

The giant catfish does not have teeth but it can still bite. It swallows its food whole and can snap up ducks or even small dogs. It is popular with fishermen because they like to eat it.

▲ Catfish will bite anything that passes, including humans.

Pikes

Pikes are fierce hunters. They live in rivers and eat fish, birds, and small mammals.

They even bite people's fingers and toes if they get the chance.

They can grow to 1.5 metres (5 feet) long.

► The snakefish is long enough to coil itself up.

Snakefish

Snakefish are like eels. They grow to over a metre (3 feet) long and have large mouths with sharp teeth.

They usually live in Asia and Africa but, in 2002, snakefish were found in the United States. They mysteriously turned up in Crofton Pond, Maryland.

Snakefish are **predators** and eat a lot of other fish. They also eat frogs, birds, and small mammals. They can crawl over land like eels and **survive** out of water for a few days.

Beware!

The largest pikes are called muskies (below). They live in North America and will attack anything that comes near.

In 1995, a tiger muskie took a bite out of a boy's wrist when he was swimming in Lake Rebecca, Minnesota.

prey animal that is killed and eaten by other animals

Piranha fact file

There are more than 20 types of piranha. Some piranhas are **vegetarian**. Other piranhas are **cannibals**. They will eat their own young.

Piranhas

There are stories of piranhas fiercely attacking people in the water. The fish strip all the flesh off people's bones in a few minutes. Fortunately, such things happen mostly in horror movies.

Even so, South American fishermen have to be careful. Many have lost toes or fingers as they wade in the river.

► The name piranha means "tooth fish". They have very sharp teeth.

cannibal animal that eats other animals of the same species

Red-bellied piranhas are the scariest fish in this family. They swim in a group called a **shoal**, looking for **prey**. As soon as they sense blood in the water, they seem to go crazy in a **feeding frenzy**. Piranhas eat sick or weak animals that fall into the water. They keep the river clean and stop disease from spreading.

Man-eater

In Africa, every year a few people are killed by bull sharks (below).

These fierce fish are as long as a small car. They have even attacked boats.

feeding frenzy wild excitement over food

The biggest

The biggest white shark ever killed was caught in 1945 near Cuba.

It was as long as a bus (6.4 metres) (about 20 feet), and it weighed 3312 kilograms (7300 pounds).

Kings of the sea

People fear sharks. Humans kill 100 million sharks every year. Many of these are killed to keep sharks away from the beaches for tourists. Yet sharks attack only about 100 people each year and fewer than half of these die from the attacks.

Great white sharks attack more people than any other sharks do. They may think swimmers and surfers are seals.

◄ When sharks lose teeth, they grow new ones.

Tiger sharks

The tiger shark lives in warm seas. It has a blunt snout and stripes on its back. Tiger sharks attack a few people each year. They will eat anything from seals and turtles to seabirds, sea snakes, and other sharks.

Fishermen have found all sorts of things inside tiger sharks, including ships' anchors and car number plates!

Tiger of the sea

The barracuda is a fierce hunter. It has sharp teeth and is called the 'tiger of the sea'.

Barracudas can grow to nearly 2 metres (6 feet) long – about as tall as a human.

◀ The stripes give tiger sharks their name.

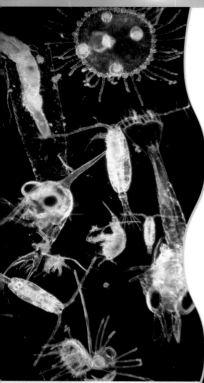

Gentle giants

The whale shark is the biggest fish in the world. It weighs as much as six elephants. Whale sharks live in deep, warm seas and often swim near the surface. They are gentle creatures and do not harm people.

Whale sharks are **filter feeders**. They swim slowly, sucking up water full of **plankton** and fish. They pump water out through their **gills**. These act like filters to trap the food.

Plankton

Whale sharks and many other **species** feed on plankton. It is like a soup of tiny plants, animals, and the eggs and young of crabs and fish. The picture above shows plankton highly magnified.

plankton tiny animals and plants floating on the surface

Basking sharks often feed near the Cornish coast in England.

Basking sharks

The basking shark is the second biggest fish in the world. Like the whale shark, it is a gentle filter feeder. It may take in 1.5 million litres of water in an hour.

The whale shark usually stays alone. Basking sharks sometimes gather in groups of over a hundred. They live in the Atlantic and Pacific Oceans and are also seen off European coasts.

Krill

One of the ingredients in the plankton 'soup' is **krill**. Filter feeders eat thousands of these tiny creatures every day.

There are millions of krill in the oceans. Scientists think that together they weigh more than all the humans on Earth.

Breeding

Fish have a strong **instinct** to produce young. They spend a lot of energy finding a **mate**.

Displaying

Some fish perform dancing displays. Others just show off their beautiful, bright colours. Down in the deep sea where it is dark, the lanternfish shine their lights to attract a mate.

Splash

The female splash tetra leaps out of the river to lay her eggs on leaves. The male leaps out to fertilize them.

He keeps the eggs wet by splashing them. They take three days to hatch.

The male splash tetra flicks water with his tail to keep the eggs wet.

Lantern fish use lights to find each other in the deep, dark water.

Mating

Most female fish lay eggs. The male swims alongside. He releases his **sperm** to **fertilize** the eggs. Some kinds of fish egg **hatch** in a day. Others take months.

Female guppies and sharks keep their fertilized eggs inside their bodies. The young hatch inside their mother and are born as live fish.

Can you believe it?

Cod lay 8 million eggs at a time. This is nowhere near as many as the ocean sunfish. She lays up to 50 million eggs at a time. They are so tiny they would all fit in this "o".

▲ The sunfish lies near the surface of the sea. It looks as if it is sunbathing.

fertilize when a sperm joins an egg to form a new living thing

Fish ladders

Some rivers have **dams** that are too high for salmon to leap.

Fish ladders are built beside the dam (see below, on the right). The salmon can swim up these on their journey back to their spawning grounds.

Salmon's leap for life

Salmon swim incredible distances to **mate** and lay their eggs. Adults live in the Atlantic and Pacific oceans. At **breeding** time they swim up rivers. Each salmon heads back to the exact stream where it first hatched.

It is a long and dangerous journey. Sometimes salmon have to leap up waterfalls. Many are caught by bears and eagles.

dam wall built to hold back water

When the salmon arrive at the **spawning ground**, they dig a nest in the gravel and **spawn**. They are worn out by their journey and soon die.

The newly-hatched salmon stay put for a while. When they have grown bigger, they make the long journey down to the sea. Like their parents, they will return to their birthplace to spawn and die.

Incredible journey

Freshwater eels live in rivers and lakes. But they travel to the Sargasso Sea, near Florida, to spawn.

The young swim to the rivers their parents came from.

◄ Grizzly bears catch salmon leaping up a waterfall.

spawn lay and fertilize eggs

Did you know?

Newborn seahorses must rise straight to the surface of the water. They gulp in air to fill their **swim bladder**. This allows them to float.

Seahorses are usually partners for life.

Seahorses

Seahorses are most unusual fish. It is the male who gives birth. The female lays between 100 and 200 eggs in the male's pouch.

The male **fertilizes** them and carries them for several weeks until they are ready to hatch. He feeds them with juices made by his body.

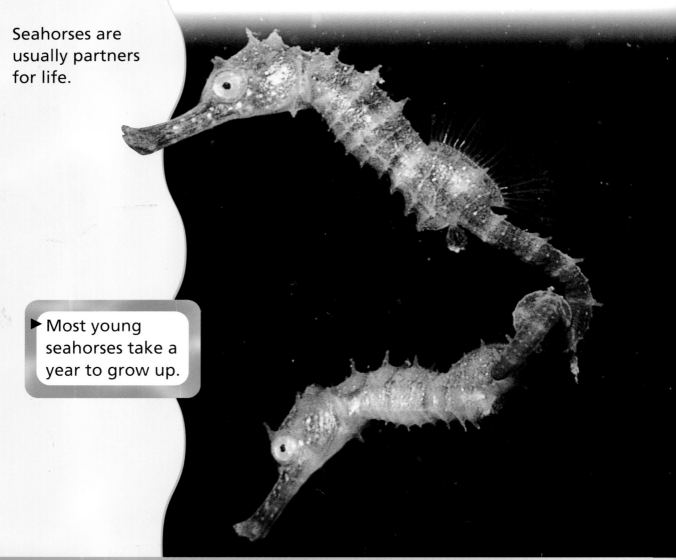

► Most young seahorses take a year to grow up.

swim bladder air sac inside bony fish that stops them from sinking

It can take two days for all the young seahorses to be born. The male squeezes them out of his pouch. He is very tired when he has finished.

The newborn seahorses may be tiny, but they can take care of themselves right away.

Pipefish

The pipefish (above) is a relative of the seahorse. He also has a long **snout** and no teeth.

The male keeps the eggs in his pouch until they are ready to be born.

◀ Baby seahorses are being born from this male's pouch.

Defence

Kill or cure

The electric torpedo ray (below) can give a 220-volt shock which stuns its prey.

In Roman times, doctors strapped a live ray to a patient's head. It was meant to cure headaches!

There are a lot of **predators** in the water. Some fish have developed a very good defence – electricity.

Livewires

Electric eels are quiet fish, but never stroke one! They can shoot out over 600 volts of electricity. A socket at home will only give 240 volts and that is enough for a very bad shock. The eels will only give a shock when they fear an attack.

They also use electricity to stun their **prey**. This makes it easier to swallow their food whole.

sensor sensitive part of the body that picks up signals

Electric eels can sometimes shoot out as much as 800 volts of electricity. That is enough to kill a horse. The eel has electric cells in its tail, that charge up like a big battery.

Electric eels find their way by sending out signals that make a kind of electric photo. **Sensors** along their body "read" the photo. It guides them through the murky waters of the Amazon River Basin.

High voltage
The electric catfish lives in freshwater in Africa. It keeps predators away with a quick zap of 350 volts. It also uses its electrical power to stun prey.

▼ Some electric eels can grow to almost 3 metres long.

▼ An electric catfish can only share an aquarium with its own young. Other fish would die from electric shock.

Lionfish

The lionfish does not need to hide. Predators can see its poisonous spines.

People usually **survive** its painful jab. But the venom makes them feel sick for days.

Deadly

Some small fish keep **predators** away by tasting horrible or having **venom**. Some fish, including stonefish and surgeonfish, have sharp spikes as well.

Stonefish lie on the seabed around Australia. Their spikes protect them from being eaten by sharks. They can badly injure a swimmer who steps on them.

► The lionfish lives in the Great Barrier Reef in Australia.

venom poison

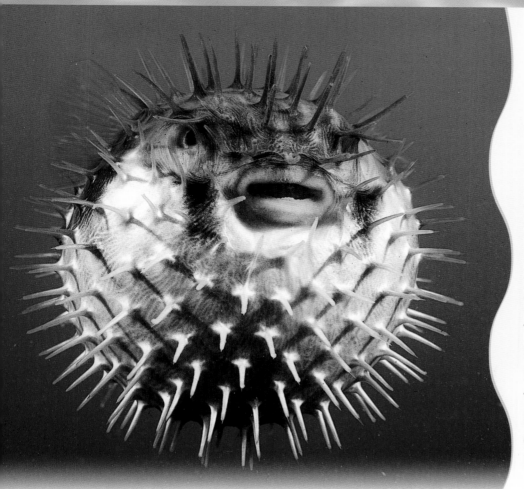

Zebrafish

The innocent-looking zebrafish is actually deadly to predators. It has poison **glands** at the base of its fins.

Pufferfish

The pufferfish gulps water when it is threatened. This makes it puff up like a ball to more than twice its normal size. It has spines as sharp as a porcupine's, making it hard for a predator to bite it.

The pufferfish also has **venom** inside its body. People have died from eating it.

Hide and seek

Some young fish have a really safe place to hide – inside their mother's mouth.

All **species** of mouthbrooders protect both eggs and young fish in this way.

Hiding

Many fish hide from **predators** by using **camouflage**. Some have colours that blend in with the background. Others can turn sideways and almost disappear because their bodies are flat.

Flatfish cannot swim fast to escape. But they can hide. Some flatfish can change colour to match the stones on the seabed beneath them.

▲ Some male mouthbrooders look after their young.

Nooks and crannies

Moray eels hide in nooks and crannies in rocks. Only their eyes can be seen. At night, they leave their dens to hunt.

It is impossible for predators to get at them in their dens. But morays can shoot out to catch passing fish. Chain morays have golden, chain-like patterns that camouflage their movements as they **slither** around in search of crabs.

Smelly jelly

At night, some parrotfish (above) cover themselves with a sort of jelly. It hides their smell, so predators will not sniff them out.

The parrotfish can get a good night's sleep in the **coral reef**. They know they cannot be found.

◄ Plaice are hard to see on the seabed.

coral reef ridge in warm seas that is make of the skeletons of millions of tiny sea animals

Weird and wonderful

Beat this

A flying fish beats its tail 50 times per second to get enough speed for take-off.

It can keep gliding for nearly a minute before it has to come down again.

Fish that fly

Flying fish don't really fly at all. They skim along the surface of the sea, beating their tails. This gives them enough speed to lift right above the sea and glide. They can glide up to 180 metres (200 yards) at a time.

Why do flying fish glide instead of swimming? Simple. It is faster. This means they can escape from dolphins, tuna, and other **predators**.

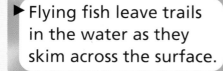

▶ Flying fish leave trails in the water as they skim across the surface.

Sometimes flying fish land on the decks of ships and get stranded. Sailors in the Volvo Ocean Race in 2002 were amazed when flying fish leapt out of the water and crashed into them at 64 kilometres (40 miles) per hour. A number of sailors were thumped in the chest and knocked over by them.

Dangerous

Leaping fish can be dangerous. In 1988, a man in Sri Lanka was killed by a garfish (below). It leapt out of the sea and speared his neck.

Shark friend

The remora fish makes a deal with the shark (below). The remora eats parasites on the shark.

In return, the shark acts as bodyguard to the little fish. The remora also eats the shark's left-over food.

Fish friends

There are at least 45 **species** of small fish that act as cleaners for larger fish. The sea wrasse is one of the busiest cleaners. It eats all sorts of **parasites** from the **gills** and mouths of large meat-eaters.

Another little fish has learnt to copy the wrasse. This "false cleaner" will pretend to clean. Then it will suddenly bite a chunk from the bigger fish's fins.

parasite animal or plant that lives in or on another living thing

Doctor fish

The Turkish kangal fish gives other fish a sort of massage. This is why it is called the doctor fish. It also nibbles dead **scales,** and skin. The doctor fish has helped humans too. Patients with diseased skin sit in a tub full of kangal fish and get nibbled. Many people say it really works!

The clownfish (above) lives among the stinging **tentacles** of the **sea anemone**. The clownfish covers itself in slime. This protects it from the stings. It is safe from **predators** that do not want to get stung.

◀ A wrasse hops into a coral trout's mouth to give it a clean.

sea anemone an animal that sticks itself to rocks and catches prey with its many tentacles

43

Hot and cold

The pupfish lives in hot springs in California, in North America. The temperature is a steamy 40 °C.

The Alaskan blackfish lives in freezing water. It can even survive -20 °C for thirty minutes.

Blood-suckers

Hagfish and lampreys feed on the blood of other fish, and may sometimes kill them. They are **parasites**. They do not have jaws. They have a soft mouth that sucks onto the fish.

Lampreys are found in rivers in North America. They will also attach themselves to humans, but they can be pulled off.

▲ A pupfish feels at home in hot water.

The fisher

The strange-looking, deep sea anglerfish lives deep down in the sea where it is very dark. It has a rod on its head with a light at the tip. This light attracts fish.

The anglerfish waits until fish come close. Then it snaps them up with its huge mouth. It can swallow **prey** larger than itself. It has a very stretchy stomach.

Did you know?

The Romans kept moray eels in seaside ponds. It is thought that they fed them on live slaves who did not work well.

King Henry 1st (1068–1135) probably died from eating a moray eel. Their flesh can be **toxic**.

◄ In the dark waters of the deep sea, prey only see the anglerfish's light. It is just as well they cannot see its face!

Fish in danger

The Great Barrier Reef

This is the biggest structure ever built by living things. It is 1600 kilometres (1000 miles) long. It is the only living structure that can be seen from the Moon.

Many fish are being affected by **pollution**. Oceans, rivers, and lakes are becoming more polluted. Fish become ill or even die.

Coral reefs

About a third of all fish **species** live in **coral reefs**. Coral reefs are one of the richest **habitats** on Earth. Coral is made up of tiny animals that are a bit like small **sea anemones.** The animals join with others to make forests of coral reef. The reefs are home to about 3 million different species of animal. Coral is being killed by pollution.

pollution damage caused by chemicals, fumes, and rubbish

Seahorses under threat

Coral reefs are also home to species of brightly-coloured seahorses. Seahorses living on the reefs are threatened by fishing.

Twenty million seahorses are caught each year. In some countries they are used to make medicines. The number of seahorses has dropped by 50 per cent in the last ten years. These amazing animals are now at great risk.

Captured

The beautiful mandarin fish (above) lives on **algae** that grow on the coral reef. These tiny fish are only 20–50 millimetres (1–2 inches) long. Many colourful reef fish are caught and sold for aquariums. This could make them **extinct** in the wild.

◄ Masses of colourful fish live in coral reefs.

algae types of simple plant without proper stems or leaves. Most grow in water or on rocks.

Threatened

Southern bluefin tuna has nearly been fished to **extinction**. It is very popular in Japan. One large fish weighing about 900 kilograms can fetch more than $US 10,000.

Endangered fish

The spotted handfish has fins like hands. Spotted handfish were quite common in Tasmania, Australia, until the 1980s.

Then people brought Northern Pacific seastars to the area. Spotted handfish numbers dropped rapidly. By 2001 there were only a few left. **Naturalists** think this may be because the starfish eat the spotted handfish's eggs.

naturalist person who studies plants and animals

The beluga sturgeon is caught for its eggs. They are made into very expensive caviar. A tiny jar, weighing as much as a small bar of chocolate, costs over £60.

The beluga has swum in the Caspian Sea in Russia since the time of the dinosaurs. It is now **endangered**. Too much fishing has cut the number of belugas by ninety per cent since the 1980s.

◄ The spotted handfish is now protected.

Very rare

A very rare cave catfish lives only in one dark cave in Namibia. The water level in the area is dropping. If the cave dries up, these catfish could disappear forever.

Over-fishing

In the 1960s 80,000 tonnes of bluefin tuna were caught every year. Now there are 90 per cent fewer tuna than in 1970 – but more people eating tuna sandwiches. Tuna may disappear from the menu before long.

Save our seas

Over 97 per cent of all life on Earth lives in the oceans. But we are poisoning the seas with **pollution**.

Another big problem is too much fishing. We take out tonnes of fish from our seas and oceans every day. Fish are caught before they are old enough to **breed**. This means there will be no young to replace them.

environment natural surroundings

Pollution

Many chemicals are **polluting** the oceans. Some are dumped on purpose. Others leak into the sea from the land and from rivers. Some pollution is making fish **infertile**. This means they can no longer produce young.

It is important that we take more care of the **environment**. Protecting the oceans for fish will also be good for people.

What can we do?

Take an interest in what is going on in our oceans. Find out about groups like the Marine Conservation Society. Help cut down pollution by 'thinking green'. Saving energy and recycling make for a healthier planet.

▼ Oil spills from tankers poison the water.

---

infertile unable to produce young

Find out more

Websites

BBC Nature
Website packed with games and quizzes to find out about all aspects of nature.
www.bbc.co.uk/ nature/blueplanet

Enchanted Learning
Information about all sorts of incredible creatures.
www.enchanted learning.com/ subjects

Marine Conservation Society
Lots of information about fish and sea mammals. It also tells you how they are protecting them.
www.mcsuk.org

Books

From Egg to Adult: The Life Cycle of Fish, Richard and Louise Spilsbury (Heinemann Library, 2003)
How Fish Swim, Jill Bailey (Franklin Watts, 2003)
Wild Predators! Killer Fish, Andrew Solway (Heinemann Library, 2004)

World wide web

If you want to find out more about fish, you can search the Internet using keywords like these:

- coelacanth
- fossil +fish
- "hammerhead shark"

You can also find your own keywords by using headings or words from this book. Use the following search tips to help you find the most useful websites.

Search tips

There are billions of pages on the Internet. It can be difficult to find exactly what you are looking for. These tips will help you find useful websites more quickly:

- Know what you want to find out about
- Use simple keywords
- Use two to six keywords in a search
- Only use names of people, places, or things
- Put double quote marks around words that go together, for example "bat ray"

Where to search

Search engine
A search engine looks through millions of website pages. It lists millions of sites that match the words in the search box. You will find the best matches are at the top of the list, on the first page.

Search directory
A person instead of a computer has sorted a search directory. You can search by keyword or subject and browse through the different sites. It is like looking through books on a library shelf.

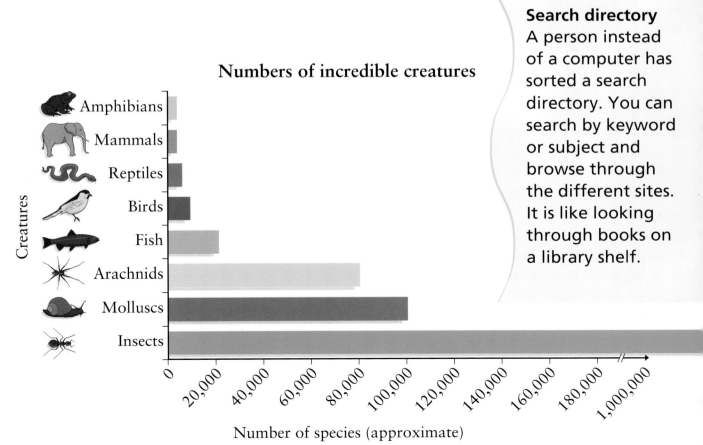

Numbers of incredible creatures

Creatures (y-axis): Amphibians, Mammals, Reptiles, Birds, Fish, Arachnids, Molluscs, Insects

Number of species (approximate) (x-axis): 0, 20,000, 40,000, 60,000, 80,000, 100,000, 120,000, 140,000, 160,000, 180,000, 1,000,000

Glossary

algae types of simple plant without proper stems or leaves. Most grow in water or on rocks.

ancestor relative that lived a long time ago

breed to produce young

camouflage colours and patterns that match the background

cannibal animal that eats other animals of the same species

coral reef ridge in warm seas that is made of the skeletons of millions of tiny sea animals

dam wall built to hold back water

endangered in danger of dying out

environment natural surroundings

extinct died out, never to return

feeding frenzy wild excitement over food

fertilize when a sperm joins an egg to form a new living thing

filter feeder animal that takes water into its body and strains out tiny pieces of food

fossil remains of a plant or animal that lived a very long time ago

gills flaps on the side of a fish's head that are used for breathing

gland special organ in the body

grazer animal that feeds only on plants

gristle strong, slightly bendy material, often called cartilage

habitat natural home of an animal or plant

hatch come out from an egg

infertile unable to produce young

instinct way of behaving that comes naturally

krill tiny, shrimp-like animals

mammal animal that produces milk to feed its young

mate partner of the opposite sex. Together they produce young.

naturalist person who studies animals and plants

oxygen one of the gases in air and water that all living things need

parasite animal or plant that lives on or in another living thing

plankton tiny animals and plants floating on the surface

poacher someone who kills and steals wild animals, although it is against the law

pollute to make air, water, or land dirty or dangerous

pollution damage caused by chemicals, fumes, and rubbish

predator animal that kills and eats other animals

prey animal that is killed and eaten by other animals

receptor part of the body that responds to a signal

scales small bony plates that protect the skin on fish and reptiles

scavenger animal that feeds on scraps and the prey of other animals

sea anemone animal that sticks itself to rocks and catches prey with its many tentacles

sensor sensitive part of the body that picks up signals

shoal group of fish

slither slide along like a snake

snout nose

spawn lay and fertilize eggs

spawning ground special place where fish go to lay their eggs

species type of living animal or plant

sperm male sex cell

streamlined smoothly shaped to move easily through water

survive stay alive despite danger and difficulties

swim bladder air sac inside bony fish that stops them from sinking

tentacle body part that is like a long, thin, bendy arm

toxic poisonous

waterproof does not let in water

vegetarian does not eat meat

venom poison

Index

Titles in the *Freestyle Express*: *Incredible Creatures* series include:

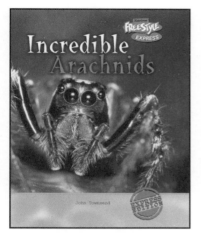

Hardback: 1844 434516

Hardback: 1844 434524

Hardback: 1844 434532

Hardback: 1844 434540

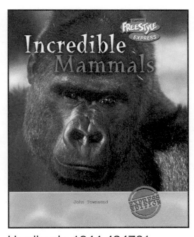

Hardback: 1844 434761

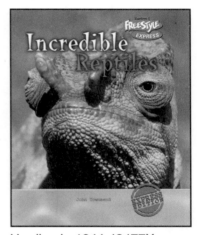

Hardback: 1844 43477X

Hardback: 1844 435172

Hardback: 1844 435180

Find out about other Freestyle Express titles on our website www.raintreepublishers.co.uk